"This collection took me deep into my soul and out into the
gift from Patty's heart to ours. To be touched in such a deep
this time of personal and collective turmoil, is a wonderful thing…"

Caryn Levin McCloskey, Spiritual Approaches to Personal Growth

In these poetic meditations, Patty Joslyn invites the reader to "wake up and love" the world and everything in it. "In my soul lives a bird," she says. "One tiny creature with nothing but a song." Her words are rich with sensory images: remembered smells (bread baking, lemon, wild mint); the feel of a communion wafer pressed against the roof of the mouth; the sight of a fence "waiting for paint or winter," children playing in puddles, the brushed strands of hair she offers to birds for their nests. Always she comes back to the love that connects all things to the divine.

Maureen Eppstein, author of *Earthward*

"This collection of distilled prose poems inspires, delights, and provokes. Joslyn's writing is sometimes fierce, sometimes whimsical, but always deeply true."

Jody Gehrman, author of *Watch Me*

When Patty Joslyn spreads her word-wings, it's as though she is not merely creating poems but mapping constellations, turning the divine night sky into something even more spectacular and also mysterious. In Joslyn's work I find enrichment for my own widening sense of wonder. I am grateful for this abundance of reasons to stay awake to joy as well as sorrow, and to honor loss alongside grace.

Elizabeth Rosner, author of *Electric City, Gravity*

Patty Joslyn's soulful voice sweeps me into a world of memories that I could swear were my own. Her words speak of the universal; love, loss, and the tenderness of a life lived with an open heart.

Rita Murphy, author of *Night Flying, Harmony*

# ru·mi·nate

## Meditations on Mystical Wisdoms

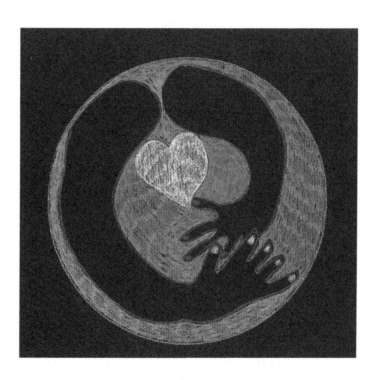

First published IngramSpark 2017


Copyright © Patty Joslyn, 2017
22pearls@gmail.com


Printed in the United States of America


Set in Palatino Linotype and Plato
Designed by Patty Joslyn and Karl Moeller


permission to use the index of first lines from
LOVE POEMS FROM GOD
was given exclusively to Patty Joslyn
from Daniel Ladinsky


Art by Patty Joslyn

ISBN 978-0-692-82310-1

# ru·mi·nate

## Meditations on Mystical Wisdoms

### Patty Joslyn

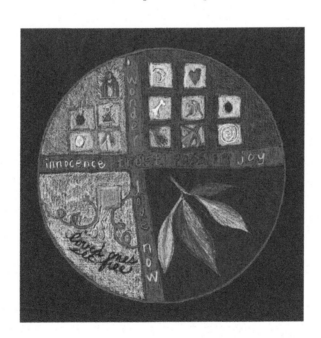

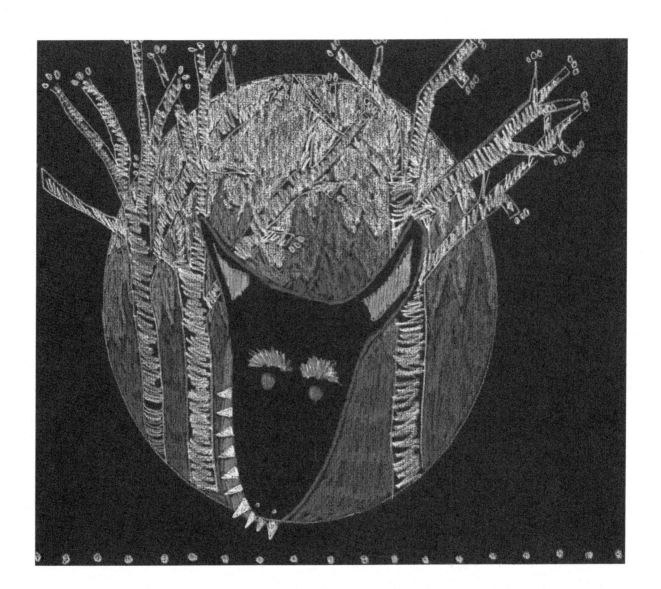

I give great thanks and acknowledgment to the wonderful work and words of Daniel Ladinsky. His bestselling Penguin anthology, *Love Poems from God: Twelve Sacred Voices from the East and West* was (and is) of great inspiration in the writing of this book. I have quoted verbatim from nearly three hundred of the first-lines of the poems in that book. What I have quoted is presented in this book in *italic,* and is the *first line or words* in each verse.

In that anthology Hafiz says, slightly rendered here by Daniel:

> I am a hole in a flute that the Christ's breath moves
>    through, listen, O listen my dear to this wondrous music.
>    – Hafiz

And may some *divine jazz* sing out and embrace you from every page here—that my heart wrote.

Patricia (Patty) Joslyn

## ...and more thanks

Oh, how my thanks grow; like the sweet peas in this past season's garden; abundance filling more vessels than I knew I housed. Overflowing thanks and love are offered to family and friends literally from *sea to shining sea*, but since Vermont doesn't yet have its own ocean I also include *there ain't no mountain high enough* to try and say it all.

I've been with these meditations and musing (and they with me) for many years. I think of them as silent chants, fortunes hanging from tea bags, unexpected love letters. They were gifts to me and now the hope is in re-gifting a heart will open a wee bit wider and we'll each find and know and remember the very thing we love about one another. It still seems to be the best medicine ever created.

With mine. xo

The drawings in this book represent many years of my work with mandalas as prayers and intentions to and through the Great Spirit of Love. Sweet gratitude to Caryn Levin McCloskey for holding this circle in the highest of light. The cover photograph I took one fine morning in my front yard. It's a grand thing; this thing called Beauty.

Kind thanks to...Karl, Maureen, Kiersten, my family and friends and you; the reader.

Extra smooches to my Dear Larry & the ones who swell my heart...

Jesse, Dylan, Thea, & Clay xo

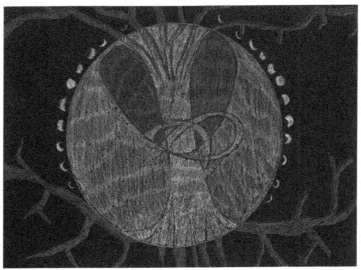

# Contents - Index of First Lines - *Love Poems From God*

*Twelve Sacred Voices from the East and West* /Daniel Ladinsky

Alphabetical ordered, (as seen in book), page number, and TITLE of poem (not used in this work)

**A**

36. Did God really call, 338, DID GOD REALLY SAY THE WORD <u>GOOFBALL</u>?

37. Do they prove anything to you, these tears?, 309, IS THAT MY FATE?

38. Does God only pucker at certain moments, 165, ONLY PUCKER AT CERTAIN MOMENTS?

39. Does God understand Himself? Not in the form of Creation, 135, DOES GOD UNDERSTAND HIMSELF?

**E**

40. Even after all this time, 170, THE SUN NEVER SAYS

41. Every creature has a religion, 128, EVERY FOOT A SHRINE

42. Every truth without exception--, 123, ON BEHALF OF LOVE

43. Everything I see, hear, touch, feel, taste, 114, EVERYTHING

**F**

44. From a distance all want to enter His house, 296, CRAZY

45. From my breath I extract God, 126, FROM MY BREATH

46. From the Ocean I hear a million fish say, 222, PROFESSIONAL COUNSELING

**G**

47. Girls, think twice before inviting God near, 254, IS ALL THIS GOOD STUFF REAL?

48. God and I have become, 171, TWO GIANT FAT PEOPLE

49. God came to my house and asked for charity, 33, HE ASKED FOR CHARITY

50. God dissolved my mind, 298, I WOULD CEASE TO BE

51. God has a special interest, 246, AND HELP HIM COMFORT

52. God has never really spoken, 343, THE SOURCE

53. God said, 336, PROBABLY VERY THERAPEUTIC

54. God sees nothing in us that He has not given, 132, WHENEVER HE LOOKS AT YOU

55. God stood at the shore of Himself and dove in, 289, MORE TRAFFIC THAN YOU THINK

76. I am always holding a priceless vase in my hands, 23, A VASE

77. I am looking for a poem that says Everything, 340, THE EVERYTHING POEM

78. I am standing naked in the marketplace, 234, KABIR, THE OIL IT BURNS

79. I asked for the most intimate experience with the Christ, 55, IN A VISION

80. I assaulted the Holy One, 335, I ASSAULTED THE HOLY ONE

81. I can't forget about love, 243, I GET DIZZY

82. I could not bear to touch God with my own hand, 106, BUT HE WANTED ME

83. I could not lie anymore, 333, FIRST HE LOOKED CONFUSED

84. I could not move against this wind if I did not pray, 16, IF I DID NOT PRAY

85. I did not have to ask, 314, THE ESSENCE OF DESIRE

86. I don't think there is such a thing, 221, AN INTELLIGENT RICH PERSON

87. I felt in need of a great pilgrimage, 227, A GREAT PILGRIMAGE

88. I first saw God when I was a child, 183, CONSUMED IN GRACE

89. I found completeness, 272, EVERY PROPHET'S NAME

90. I had a natural passion for fine clothing, excellent food, 292, I LOVED WHAT I COULD LOVE

91. I had been asking God for a sign to help me, 233, SPECULATIVE

92. I had tea yesterday with a great theologian, 279, CLARITY IS FREEDOM

93. I had to seek the Physician, 229, I HAD TO SEEK THE PHYSICIAN

94. I have a cause, 144, OTHERWISE, THE DARKNESS

95. I have come into this world to see this, 159, I HAVE COME INTO THIS WORLD TO SEE THIS

96. I hear talk about the famous, 24, A BREAST IN THE SKY

97. I hear you singing, dear, inviting me to your limb, 44, A WEDDING GIFT

**L**

**M**

**N**

(X)/Y

Z

# ru·mi·nate

## Meditations on Mystical Wisdoms/Patty Joslyn

A

*A bird took flight* and startled me like a sneeze coming from another room. I thought I

was alone. You had gone to visit the other one. Seven boxes you loaded into the small

white car. I reminded you to use your mirrors, said it was all too much, then later I went

to lie in the very space you took the things from. He is gone I said to nobody, to myself,

the heavy humid air, and the fan blowing it all around. The place a gray floor with nail

holes and long deep scratches that still smell of him.

A *delirious gang* of hens
pecked at wet ground
clucking thanks

to small treasures
I hadn't seen

strutting to show the others
grains of nothingness
they carried
in their hardened beaks

their gnarled yellow nibs
reminded me of the toenails
on the grandmother who once knew my name
rocked me in her lap
smelled of lemon and wild mint

Now the smell is almost visual
making it hard for me to breathe

*A flame* coming from a window caught the eye. When we could safely turn the car around we did. The police officer asked why we thought this a good reason. A good answer was a good deed. When we pulled into the overgrown driveway we were given sky reflecting off a pane of broken glass. You said, it just doesn't seem real.

*A good gauge of spirited health* would be to open the brown bottles lined up in the window in full sun and remember who you are and what you need. The tops of the jars are rusty and all the money spend on them can not be gotten back. Instead, hold under your tongue love and wait for it to dissolve.

*A good poem is like finding a hole* in your sock. Your favorite ones. You wonder how, why, when it happened. How much longer you should keep them around. You think of mending it, yet know the yarn will make a small bump inside and this will drive you crazy. So you save them for dusting or tie them in a tight knots and watch the dog play with these things you once loved.

*A great helplessness I felt at times* then the remainder settled into my body and mind and I laughed at myself. The communion wafer is a thin round idea. To hold it pressed against the roof of the mouth is a whole other thing.

*A hand in my soul can reach out and touch Jerusalem* and on its palms there are lines. One is called life. The man who took the Butternut Tree down, because it was dead, showed me his stained hands when he finished. Like henna, I said. The line called life was the only clean spot on his hands.

*A man born blind* hears voices I search for. He doesn't know how many colors of one thing there are. That to say blue or green means so many things. He doesn't know day-lilies wilt before they fall yet while hanging the color fades and offers itself to the dusk.

love

*A man standing* with his hands in his pockets rattling change watched the parade as it rounded the corner of State and Main. His expression never changed. Towards the end of the route eight men, dressed in blue, holding guns like I would hold a baby, are doing what I call marching. They are shouting simple words. One. Two. Left. Right. When they stop and aim the guns at the sky this is where I look. One white balloon floats by. When they shot the guns my legs felt weak. The man on the corner dropped to his knees.

*A thorn has entered your foot* and as you sit across from me working it out I remember, again, that your eyes are the color of wet amber. A resin, like pitch, that sticks even to itself. It leaves the tree as slow as a heart beat. I want to look at you for a long time. As you sit with the thin shiny sliver in your hand it is me with tears.

*A tool in your hand I am, dear God* use me as you will. Find my right work. My right place like a hook in a big barn. The barn needs a coat of paint. The hook holds me in place until I am needed. I am waiting for you to call.

*A woman and her young daughter were destitute* but they didn't know it. They looked at me and smiled. Me, the one judging something else. Their eyes were liquid, their devotion the very thing I pray for. It's as if I am sitting here beside a river searching to find something to quench my thirst.

*A woman's body, like the earth, has seasons*
And though I sit in the heat of July
I am in the autumn of my life
A time of harvest and release
Shorter days of sunlight
Branches let go of what they hold
Colors muted and blurred
Winter will come.


*Admit something* to me; tell me about the night I was away and the woman with the long

dark hair came to visit. She lit candles, the ones you hate the smell of. She touched you

and you spoke of me. Admit her hands didn't understand the word no. Her lips

answered questions you asked. Admit you were weak, she was strong. Other things got

in the way of decision. Admit this house is green. The vines growing up the maple tree

are slowly killing it; if it were to fall we would both be dead.


*All are having a relationship with God:* The bread in the oven rising with warmth. The

flower of the hostas reaching towards the light. Water rushing against the river's banks.

A bird with one seed in its mouth, after it swallows it will again know to sing.

*All beings are words of God* and words are everywhere.
Stick. Grass. Leaf. Bird. Bee. Red barn.
Each sunflower seed cracked and left behind.
The fence waiting for paint or winter.
Blue sky. White puffy clouds.
A peak of a ridge line holding its own place,
almost movable,
almost forever.

*All day long a little burro labors*
ready to push out a new life.
I think of the hooves tucked inside her womb,
kicking their way into the world.
The few short breaths the new one will take
and how soon it will stand on its own.
I think of the hooves of my own children,
their tiny hands,
the somersaults they did inside of me.
How long it took them to stand,
then walk away.

*All has been consecrated*
and now it's time for the
forgiving

in the church I was in
yesterday
I looked around for the box
called confessional

imagined the stories told on bent knees
the loin of velvet
hanging between
incense and yesterdays

I remembered a time long ago

my back to the door
whispering a prayer
to the unseen woman
named Mary

full of grace

*All of what I would want my children to know* they already hold within. I tell them of fast cars and slow decisions. The good aunts and the bad. I remind them to chew, to brush, to wipe from the front. I offer treats: tapioca, roasted sweet potatoes, cocoa in their birthday cake. I tell stories. Secrets. Dreams. I sing to them while dancing, rocking, almost asleep. I know they know love and this makes me smile.

*All these miracles are about to drive me crazy.* Whose line is this?

Was it a movie, a song, or the words my mother said to my dad?

*All these things desire to be like god:* leftover rain gathered into puddles, reflection of clouds as they lie themselves down in shallow mirages of memories. Mud the color of fine Spanish skin, the pools of her eyes, and the soles of her flat lovely feet.

*Always from the child's hand* are gifts honest and open. A small, clutched, dirty hand opens; inside a minted moth wing broken into jeweled slices of flight.

*Anxious to see you, I died to the world* and with my first breath you were light. You, the swollen breast that fed and nourished me. Yours, the arms that held me pressed against your beating heart.

*Ask anything* anything at all. Why I wear a wooden mustache dangling from a cord against my chest? Why my right leg drags across the floor following me like death? Why do I look up when a plane flies over? Why I see colors left behind? And why are there tears running down my face?

*At last the time came for the bride* to say the words that would tie her to you. The silence was deafening and elongated. It allowed all who were witness a moment to know and remember the power of the heart.

B

*Because of my compassion, the sun wanted to be near me all night*
And now as it splashes itself across a darkening sky
Music and voices mingle
I know the connection of all
I cry listening to a young couple in front of me
Them getting to know one another and themselves
His smile lighting up the moment
Her quiet eyes drinking him in
Still, it's the setting sun that calls me home.

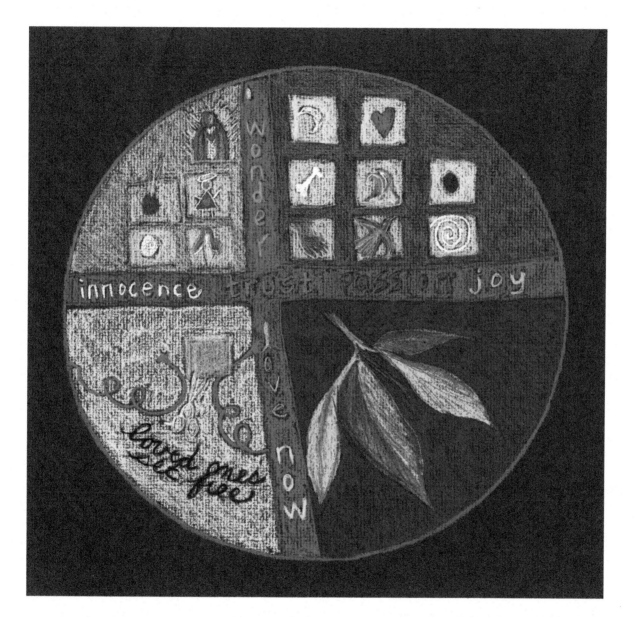

*Because the woman I love lies inside of you,*
I know and remember my name
I put letters down on a piece of paper
And say I love you
I add an x and an o
And hope you feel the ways we cross and connect
A web that holds a spider
A vine that welcomes her flowers.

*Before I fell asleep last night* I called out your name. It was a whisper in a dark room. The echo came back and laid itself on my eyelids. All night the weight kept me flat. The love kept me here.

*Birds don't brag about flying* and neither would I. I look down from a point between me and the air each holding one another as if I were my other hand or yours. The simple way two things fit together to become one.

C

*Can true humility and compassion exist in our words and eyes* as we cry sobs of distress and loneliness. Can you understand the way I hope and wish to reach you? Then you, of all people, reach across the void, and offer the last thing you have. It opens my eyes, my heart and causes me to weep.

*Capable of the universe are your arms* around me. I raise my head to howl at an afternoon where and when I know how far away I am from the ultimate, my departure. How is it I can not save you and you can not touch me. A sadness deep within unlocks as I search for the rusty key.

*Certainty undermines one's power* as if anything could be a plan grander than the ultimate, the one with no human words wrapped around. No set dates or times. As the morning opens itself to a new day we foolishly look at the clock and think it is time.

*Commerce is supported by keeping the individual at odds* with themselves, with others, with what could, or might, or should, or will be traded. An exchange of flat paper for shoes, wine, a shiny new car, a diamond necklace. Commerce is the thing you wear around your neck and yet nobody sees it.

D

*Daybreak* splits the sky into pieces. I stand at the water's edge and call it beautiful.

*Dear God, please reveal to us* the last missing piece of the puzzle we long to complete so we can run our hands against the smooth and shiny surface before crumbling it and fitting it back into its small box, the one that will be sheltered for another to complete. Testing patience and vision, while hunched over another idle hobby or obsession. Allow me to take it all apart before it begins.

*Did God really call,* was my volume turned off, or my mailbox full, or did I hit ignore. I thought it was the other one, the one I could call mother, the one who knows me just as well.

*Do they prove anything to you, these tears* of first love, these words saying I will do anything forever. Do you know they could not possibly be true; my words, handed to me from the ones who have walked the same road so many times their shoes are full of holes.

*Does God only pucker at certain moments* like with the lime juice in my glass, or the bitter fruit I bit into thinking something else. Or the way words sit in my mouth held against a line of teeth closed tight.

*Does God understand himself? Not in the form of creation* that I carry around with me each and every day but instead as the wind, the fog, the dream that woke me and made me call out to you.

E

*Even after all this time* I sometimes forget your name. I forgot I don't need it to call out.

I forget you haven't gone anywhere, that you live behind my eyes and within my

worried heart. When I speak to you the sun grows warmer and birds sing in joy.

*Every creature has a religion,*
to the birds it is first light.
I marvel at their sharing as they flit away.

I have taken to brushing my hair outside,
thin gray and gold strands
I offer the birds.

I imagine whole nests spun of love and thanks.

*Every truth without exception* carries with it a lie. Interpretation changes as soon as the words are spoken. It's silence that knows truth. The loneliness of self, the only place the beloved dares to live.

*Everything I see, hear, touch, feel, taste* is bigger than me. If I am awake and whole I know the source as you, as light that surrounds me. A halo of perfection. Of these things I want I am not ashamed.

F

*From a distance all want to enter his house* but as death comes closer we think—later. Not quite yet. I have these ones. I love her now. A list yet to explore. I have a friend who claims she loves only him, but she never wants to die. I can't tell her what I think nor can I hear her cry.

*From my breath I extract God* on the same breeze that lifts things into the high and holy air. Towels on a line, palm fronds against one another, the hair in my eyes, birds calling it home.

*From the ocean I hear a million fish say* thanks
Some fly
Others beach themselves
Their bones are looked at like art.

G

*Girls, think twice before inviting God near.* It's the same for my boys, the ones

I call my own. The same ones who flutter my heart. I say think twice, then think again,

to what it is you call your own.

*God and I have become* one. It's early morning and a silence slips in under my ribs

inviting me to close my eyes and let the voices go. There's the smell of roses,

peppermint, and another thing that is ancient and always.

*God came to my house and asked for charity.* I offered what I had. It was not much.

A banana, a cup of tea, some old jewelry I knew was worth its weight. When I was alone

I rubbed my wrist in the place the silver once was. It was pale and smooth and felt

lighter than before.

*God dissolved my mind* and I sang hallelujah. My head thrown back. My knees bent. My eyes closed. The light that poured in did not come from a window yet it warmed my aging bones.

*God has a special interest. God has never really spoken. God held the earth. God said* all this to no one yet we took it and preached in and for his name. I wonder what the others would say now if they knew what I know. If they felt this weight in their heart where would they rest their heads.

*God sees nothing in us that he has not given* away before. Birds have wings, stones weight, fish eyes, cats ears perked or flattened to pounce. Hungry mouths fill the planet and voices rise in scream or song. We take what we can to become what we will to hold what we want.

*God stood at the shore of himself and dove in* and I want to know how you know this, and how you know who it was? I don't think God has a gender, only a love full of light.

*God's admiration for us is indefinitely greater* than our own. A sad fact that seems to rule most humans lives and hearts after the age of what? Infant? Toddler? When is it we become separate and lesser? Why is it we question this eternal love?

*Great lions can find peace in a cage* if they are stuffed and waiting at a fair. You toss the balls or break a balloon, inside a special number of a piece of ordinary paper. You are reminded you can not have the cage as you reach for the great-maned creature that a year later you will sell at a yard sale for one dollar.

H

*Having lunch in a field one day* I watched two dragonflies play a game of tag.
One was laughing. This was the truth.

*He desired me so I came close* said the younger innocent version of me. I remember the hat he wore; a broken-in straw thing with a thin band braided from horse hair. Where the fine hair met there was pinned a gold cross, it was no bigger than a new bud on my rose bush.

*He has never left you.* It's the darkest hour that reminds and illuminates this hope. When all else falls away and sobs leave your chest there is a pressure that has no words. It's here you meet again.

*He is sweet that way.* A vision like a rainbow. In the back yard it is raining. Out front the kids are playing in puddles and wishing for their own pots of gold.

*He left his fingerprints on a glass.* Bands and circles of life. In his old age they were thin and forgotten. The mind was next to release and yet how the body kept time.

*He was too shy to sing* your praises, so he raised his voice and hand in other ways. This being human can be so very hard.

*Herbs can help the body,* tinctures of plant medicine carried in brown or blue bottles.

Taken under the tongue or held under a flannel pillow for later. The earth releases as

you trust her ways.


*Here is a relationship booster* look them in the eyes and open your heart.

Practice the words love and thanks.


*His hands can shape through ours,*
us—the clay—molding earth
to be
one
our empty hands powerful.
Open they offer possibilities and hope.
The dirt under my nails is here for a reason.


*How could I love my fellow man who tortured me* you asked. I answered you with tears

enough to water the garden you newly planted. Faith is a time not a place.

*How did the rose* know it was it's time to open. As I carried it into the kitchen one thorn took a drop of my blood, it seemed a fair trade.

*How did those priests ever get so serious* and why? Do they not know the way into us sinners is through a loud laughing backdoor?

*How humble is God* this not a question I could pretend to answer unless you are asking of

the God within me. If this is the question I would drop to my knees.


*How is it they live for eons in such harmony.* Perhaps by taking most things away. To create

a balance and to stop trying to agree on most everything.


*How long can the moth flirt*
with the pane glass window
with the light beside it
with its own reflection and death?


*How long can grown men and women*
*in this world* think they are different.
Heartbeat.
Breath.
Emotions.
Blood and birth.
Desires and death.

# I

*I am a hole in the flute,* an emptiness in a reed of wonder.

With nothing but the air in your lungs you make me sing.


*I am always holding a priceless vase in my hands* though it can not be seen.

This is the way I carry the love you gifted me. Its weight is mine alone.


*I am looking for a poem that says Everything* when I realize there are no words for the way

I feel about you. Silence washes over us both.


*I am standing naked in the marketplace* waiting to be cocooned in a wrap.

Later my wings will emerge, then I will whisper my goodbyes.

*I asked for the most intimate experience with the Christ* but you didn't understand me. You've always thought me a sinner. You saved your blessings for a sneeze. I gave mine all away.

*I assaulted the holy one* in you and now taking it back is near impossible. Your talons choose this moment to dig in the deepest. The wounds are still healing. Maybe always will be.

*I can't forget about love* though there have been times I've tried. There is no switch to this kingdom, no door that I can close.

*I could not bear to touch God with my own hand*, my own mortal, dirty claw, so I offered my heart, the one I wore on my tattered sleeve.

*I could not lie anymore* about the death of my best friend for though she was alive she was gone forever to me. I still weep to think of the unknown reasons.

*I could not move against this wind if I did not pray* and now on my knees

the breeze is too strong to stand against. With dirt in my eyes I look to the future.


*I did not have to ask* the flowers to unfold.

I did not have to ask the man at the door to go away.

I did not have to ask how much longer I should wait to know the truth.


*I don't think there is such a thing* as always or forever, except in the folds of the heart.

The rickrack of thin fabric that holds me together against a wildly beating creature

that seems to call all the shots.


*I feel in need of a great pilgrimage,* a short walk away from the sound

to the look of the ocean,

a long stroll to look in my children's eyes.


*I first saw God when I was a child* in a cloud. This too changed in a matter of time,

in the blinking of my eyes.

*I found completeness* yet when I reached to hold it it slipped through my fingers like the

water I tried to carry to your hungry mouth.


*I had a natural passion for fine clothes, excellent food* and more.

Then at the moment it was to matter I stood naked and hungry.


*I had been asking God for a sign to help me* right before I hit the floor.

Why now? I wondered.

The cold tile against my bruised face. My hands ready to hold you.


*I had tea yesterday with a great theologian.* She carried with her the scent of peppered sweet

peas and smoke. When she left I cried. I washed the two mugs in hot soapy water.

The flowers are purple.


*I had to see the physician* for help with my breath and now the deepness surprises even

me. All this time I thought it was supposed to hurt to release, hurt to take in, hurt to

begin a day.

*I have a cause* and one day soon I hope to know it. It's a passion that creates life and supports me in every way. Perhaps I am too fast in brushing lint and crumbs away.

*I have come into this world to see this* life of mine well lived and loved. There were aunts and uncles who watched from picnic tables full of food and laughter. Later the smell of wood smoke and tobacco. Now I am an aunt of many who I do not see enough of. They have grown into young adults with full lives and I wonder if they hold a space for me.

*I hear talk about the famous* and it's all the same stuff. Death. Birth. Pregnancies. The changing of roles and times. The loss or gain of weight and attention. I wonder if all the money helps in the least, if their dreams are as sweet as my own.

*I hear you singing, dear, inviting me to your limb* on the tree out front
full of ruby berries.
I offer you the hair that has loosened from my head.
I offer you thanks for your song.
I am too heavy for the branch but my voice is with you.

*I know a cure for sadness* but for you this medicine is not right. All of us with our own

dark night, no matter the time of day. All of us reaching for the one thing that will invite

peace.


*I know about love the way the fields know about light.*
The warm spreading of gold,
then the lifting that brings on the darkness.
The blanket of silence that invites the night creatures
and me.


*I know how it will be when I die,* this I say on the reminder of what could have happened.

I think of the early mornings when I cried missing you.

I wonder where I go when I sleep.


*I know the vows the sun and moon took* — the agreement of forever. I look at you in the early

morning, innocent, a new beginning. I hold my hand against your beating heart and say

again I do.

*I like when* you hold my hand while we are walking side by side. The way our footsteps find a rhythm and a way. Often we have nowhere to go, yet the journey is enlightening.

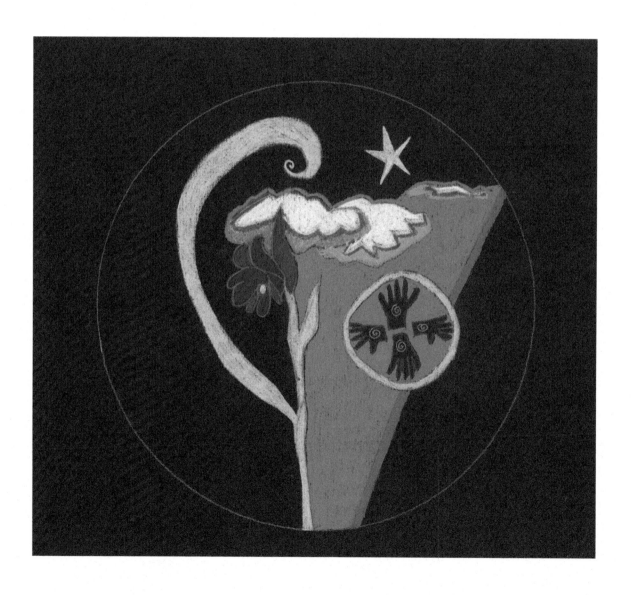

*I lived with her night and day*
wisps of memories
smells that followed me room to room.


Sometimes lilac
other times burnt cinnamon and sugar.
She was in the folds of my clothing,
the knots of my carpets,
the strands in my hair.


A shift in the wind and no sign of rain.


There was thought of other things:
wet grass
damp towels
the dog's bed
climbing roses;
sweet, pungent, and familiar.


Her name a shadow more beautiful than the flower that made it.
Her voice a bird in flight over my head.

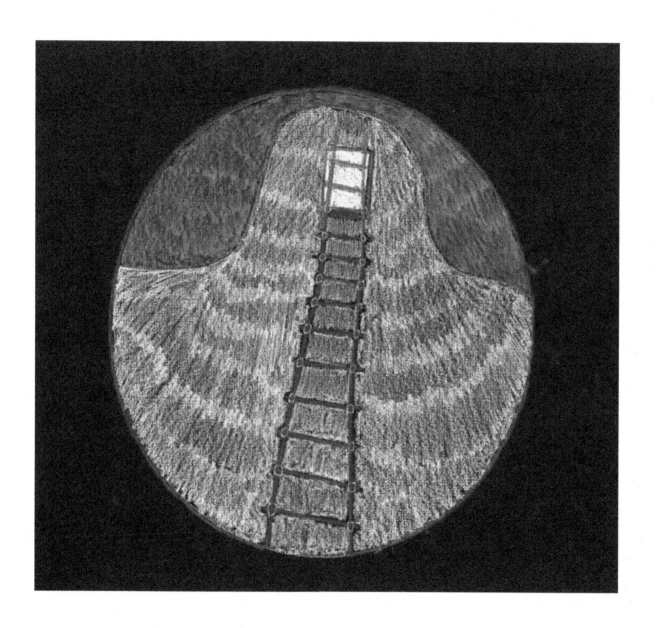

*I look at your body*
And know things it has done
Boards nailed
Buckets carried.
The people it has helped
And hugged and let go of.
One day soon your body will release tears of loss
But not until the very moment we hear the news.
Your father is dying
It is his time.
A long well-lived life
Soon he will ice skate
To places he wishes to revisit
Old countries and loved ones.


*I once spoke to my friend, an old squirrel, about the sacraments,* her chatter back to me was

full of wisdom and mirth. She laughed and said sometimes you feel like a nut. With a

chuckle we were kin.

*I remember how my mother would hold me*

at arm's length to check my gin-fizzed breath,

shake her head, and put a finger to both our mouths.

Not a word, she'd whisper, not a sound,

As I slunk down the long hallway in the early morning light.


*I said to a squirrel, what is that you are carrying,*
expecting an answer.
It's mouth full of autumn,
full of hard shelled acorns,
full of hope.


delight

*I said to God, "Let me love you."*
I said this over and over again.
I wanted to believe in the invisible mystery some call guilt.
Others call everything.
I wanted to believe in praying.
In confession.
Water to wine.
Angels.
The beautiful woman named Mary.
I wanted to believe each Hallelujah was a newly planted seed.
Let me love you seemed so innocent
Except for the plea in my voice.


*I said to God* secrets small and big. Told my sins the same.

I was asked to kneel and pray.

I was asked to tell and know the truth.

The very thing I was searching for.

So why and when the first lie?

I wish I could remember the moment I crossed the thin line

of which there seems no turning back.

*I said to Love,*
Remember me,
Please hold an eternal place for me here with you.
When all else is done and gone
I want to touch things that can't be held in the hands.


*I sat one day with a priest,* he smelled of sweat, cologne, and wine.

I looked out the stained glass windows and thought of paradise.


*I stood before a silkworm one day*
Trying to understand its work in the world
Trying to understand my own
The tangled webs we weave
To create precious lives and homes.
The day was still and yet from somewhere there was music
It filled the sounds-bird and running water
The moment opened to a pair of hummingbirds
In search of greater sweetness.

*I talk about it sometimes with him, all the suffering in the world*, the unknowns and desires to make sense of this senselessness. Suffering; a thing we each know. We call it other names, try to bury it, cover it up. It comes back the moment we open our hearts again.

*I think God gave us the wrong medicine* from the very start. An apple a day leads to more and more, always hungry, always searching for the perfect thing to sink our teeth into. Always the next meal, the next thing, always hoping to savor the last moment, the last morsel. But time has no stomach, no emotions. It simply goes on by.

*I think God might be a little prejudiced* if we think he was once a mortal being. How could this not be true? Hair color, skin color, eye color, time of day, favorite food, flower, season, state, or smell.

*I think the moon is pregnant again* her round belly pressing against a pale blue morning. A veil of a woman and time. Soon a cry will break the day and she will return to her labor while I go about mine.

*I thought of putting my hand where I could tell no one* but the ashes were hot geranium embers holding words I desired.

*I tried controlling myself but it did no good* so I called you and you answered and it wasn't easy or good. I put the phone down, walked away, and started to pull weeds, but they weren't weeds at all. So that in the morning the new seedlings were gone as were the calla lilies that had been almost as tall as me.

*I want that kind of grace from God* she whispered from behind me
I could never shush her and now she is gone
I'll never hear her voice again
Never swat her hand as if at a fly
While trying not to adore her smirk
I've known her my entire life
How many people can you say that about?

*I want to have this* moment pressed and framed, a reminder of thanks. A reminder of you beside me. A reminder we are both alive and well, if we tried to catch it or touch it, it would be like the wings of a moth, paper thin and so very fragile.

*I wanted to be a hermit and only hear the hymns* but instead a thin woman dressed in blue and black walked up to me to tell me she didn't agree with what I did not do. The music stopped and allowed me to look away. I told her of the death of your mother, the word orphan pulsating against my heart. Tomorrow I hope to practice the act and art of the hermit.

*I wanted to hold him as an infant* again, my first born
Today is his birthday, he's now thirty-seven
and I am much older
He's a wonderful-hearted man
I'm blessed to call him mine.

*I wanted to put something on this page*

But it didn't have a name
Or place or time
It was a jewel
A ruby perched upon my hat/halo
But you couldn't see
The gem sparkled like ripples on a bay
An afternoon not so long ago

*I was born for you* I whispered into your aging ear. When we both grow deaf how will you know it's me? How will I hear the sweet nothings you wake up with on your lips? What will the children do, where will they go when I scream I love you from the top of my heart?

*I was invited* into the water by elegant terns. Would I say there were a thousand or more? Their stark white bodies lined up to rest. Yet, the chatter went on and on. I've since learned they will lose the caps they wear atop their bony heads. Toss them to the wind when autumn comes closer. The very time I'd think they'd need these wonderful hats.

*I was looking for that shop,* the one with hammered brass trinkets, remembering the tiny seed beads pressed into the metal by fingers smaller than my own. I know where it was. The door, the paint faded yellow, four windows large enough for eyes to peek in. The door was locked. I knew they were gone.

*I was meditating with my cat the other day* or so I thought when it reached up to bat my face. Soft velvet pressed against my breath. I straightened my spine and the cat fell back to sleep.

*I was sad one day and went for a walk*
I found five feathers
And one sand dollar
I left them in the sand

There was a time I'd have brought them home
Lined the kitchen windowsills
with all things I'd called mine and found.

Now, I look at them and smile

*I won't go to sleep tonight until you have spoken to me.* I'll know when you slip in beside me. The weight of my own being will shift and settle. My mind will empty and ready to gather new seeds.

*I wouldn't take no for an answer*
So I don't ask the question,
Not again.
Can I die before you, please?
I no longer ask.
I have a plan on my own.

*I would not have set foot on this earth* had I known what I know now.

The witnessing of destruction.

The mindlessness of the power of money and the money of power.

Where is the balance? Who is in charge of love and light over all else?


*I would not leave this earth* to come back again.

I would not fly to the moon or go back in time.

I would not want to be anything but the mother of my children.

I would not want to be taller or fatter or shorter. I would not want bunions or bad teeth.

I would not want a fat rich husband or a mean mother. I would not want to walk on

water, though I would love to fly. I would love to know other languages and

instruments. I would love to wake from this dream and know it's not a dream.

*If all the tenderness in the world could reflect* this moment we'd all be in a better place.

*If God invited you to a party* what would you wear,
she asked. I laughed so hard my belly hurt.
Really, that's the thing you'd worry and wonder about?
I asked her.
What about questions you'd have ready?
She looked at me as if I were nuts. Maybe I am.

*If God said* jump, would you? On the high dive of your life, no water in the pool, no

lifeguards, no swimsuit or swimsuit body. Would you? How would you know the voice

if it didn't come from yourself, from a trusted loved one. Numerous phones calls and

messages saved to listen to again. Is this the voice of Love of this being called God?

*If God would stop telling jokes* I'd stop laughing at myself. I'd pick a reason and believe in

it. And me. I wouldn't have to re-invent myself. Again. I wouldn't have to wonder why

you do what you do. All the whys could slip away and we could get down to the hard

work and ways of love.

sweet thanks

*If he let go of my hand* in the dark or underwater would I survive? If he let go of my hand today or tomorrow which side of the bed would I sleep on? If he let go of my hand would I grasp for another or put my hands deep into my pockets and rub the coins as if they were wealth?

*If I did not understand* my mother then, I do now.

I wrap the shawl she has recently gifted me around my shoulders and neck.

I didn't smell her then but this morning she is with me.

Her skin like the fabric I am adorned in.

Silk and pashmina. Grey and worn. Beautiful.

It's the smell of a closet full of wishes and hopes.

It's talcum powder, wax, and a dusty wig found on a top shelf.

*If I told you the truth about God* we'd both be better off. He's a deer in a small pack at the top of the hill waiting to take flight. He's fast and fit. Antlers wrapped in velvet. Able to turn tail and never be seen again.

*If you circumambulated every holy shrine in the world*

it would bring you back here~home, to me. Why don't you?

*If you cried in Heaven* would I, could I, hear you?

Where is this place called Heaven?

Are you there or here? If you cried in Heaven the hope is that it be Joy.


*If you put your hands on this oar with me* would we find our way home?
Would we find our way back together?
Wind, waves, a thousand words
Whipped and weathered
Winded
As a million dreams
Drop
To the ocean floor.


*If you want* to know the sky say big
Say simple things under your breath
And when you stand up
Give thanks with hoots of forever
Whistle at the dogs to join you
Know they wouldn't be here forever
And neither will you or I
If you want to know more
Stop looking outside yourself.

*If your pockets were happy with coins* would I hear the jingle? Would you buy me a handful of tulips—red and yellow with hollow flimsy stems? I'd be sad when the petals opened to throw back their feathery satin things a moment ago I rubbed against my cheek.

*In my soul* lives a bird. One tiny creature with nothing but a song.

*In my travels I spent time with a great yogi* and nobody knew it but me. A man in a white vest with a terrible sense of humor. He smelled like tobacco and spent lilacs. He carried brown stains on both hands.

*In my travels I came upon a village*—dark smoke coming from stone chimneys. Water gathered in the oddest of vessels. It was the silence I was looking for. The very reason I left as fast as I could.

*In our present need for thee: Beloved, let us know your peace.*

Not a thing to be held, not a thing to be named and enough reason to find you again.


*Ironic, but one of the most intimate acts* is waking up beside my love.

No words. No before. No later. A blank sheet to call home.


*It acts like love-music*, a universal song with no words to understand.

You press the chords, touch the keys, release vibrations that echo the heart.


*It could be said that God's foot is so vast*
a print in the morning dew,
a hollow in the sand.
A pile of dirt on a hardwood floor.

*It helps* to find another place, another view.
It helps to release and relax
To know and not
To imagine a time without you.


*It is a lie*, any talk of God. Any thoughts of holding on to a belief. In two heartbeats your

world might be destroyed, then who's name will you call? What would you call prayer?


*It is your destiny to see as God sees* but with no eyes. What direction do you look?

How do you stare off into the depths of the wild ocean with vision that seeks no more?


*It was easy to love God in all that* until the baby child was taken to be no more.

Why that child? Why now? How many times can the heart be repaired?


*It's rigged*, everything in your favor, he said to his two brothers right before he slipped

and fell. Neither of them laughed. Who helped who get up was always to be the

mystery—a piece of their puzzle.

*It's an old shell trick with a twist* nothing to be had except the glazed underbelly smooth

as an ear. Holding it to your own you hear the future.

J

*Joy is the greatest cleanser and it is* never-ending.

Shadows hide in shadows at dark, always held close to the earth.

Nothing to fear, they whisper but our own hearts are beating too loud to hear.

*Just sit there right now* and know soon enough you will be called. A thousand ways to be

anywhere but here. A thousand reminders of enough. More ways to fight the battle of

being along.

*Just these two words he spoke* - Love now.

# K

*Know the true nature of your beloved* so at peace you can rest.
At night when your eyes close know the love that surrounds you.
One day it will call you to a final home.
Now it calls you to be free.

*Knowledge always deceives* the smartest of men.

They forget how to use a spoon, how to wash their own feet, how to love life.

# L

*Live with dignity, women, live with dignity, men* and let the children live with none. Allow

them to ask the fat man, why? The old woman, when? The ghosts of yesterday, who?

*Living with that guy, how could you have not gone nuts* — too loud in all ways.

Drunk off his own vinegar. Afraid of his own piss.


*Look how a mirror* reflects ugliness. While a thin pane of glass invites beauty in.


*Look what happens to the scale* when I only use one foot to guess my weight.

The needle flickers like a candle set near an open window. One gust and a step back.


*Love is* a thousand reasons to come home. It's the opening of a gate.


*Love, you have wrecked my body* so now it wants more of you. Last night I slept alone and

it wasn't right or good. It was me with bad dreams, me with the want of you. I miss the

smell of love.

M

*Maybe if I brought the moon a little closer* we could both climb atop.

You, with a fishing pole.

Me, with a poem to whisper in your ear.

Us, with hundred more years together.


*More significant than any act is the power* to forgive. And to love. Forgiveness is a fierce creature; part porcupine, part armadillo, part snake, and dark fears of murky underwater unknowns. To forgive takes one deep into their own dark well, the very place we don't want to name or visit.


*Most men in power have not the strength or wisdom* to either tip or right their own small boat. The thought of getting wet while being cradled in water not a place they want to go.

*Most poets are like a belly dancer* the circling
the need to expose the center
and yet hold it sacred and close.

*My beloved said* sweet nothings.

So I sat in silence and knew who I once was.

*My lips got lost on their way to the kiss* and though I shy away from you it isn't for the lack

of want. There is a time where nothing seems close enough. Desire becomes the bridge

to cross to the other side.

*My Lord told me a joke.*

I am still laughing.

*My perfect Lord song* out of tune, it free me from the judgment of quality.

I want to howl at the tides, moan at your touch, sing to the morning light.

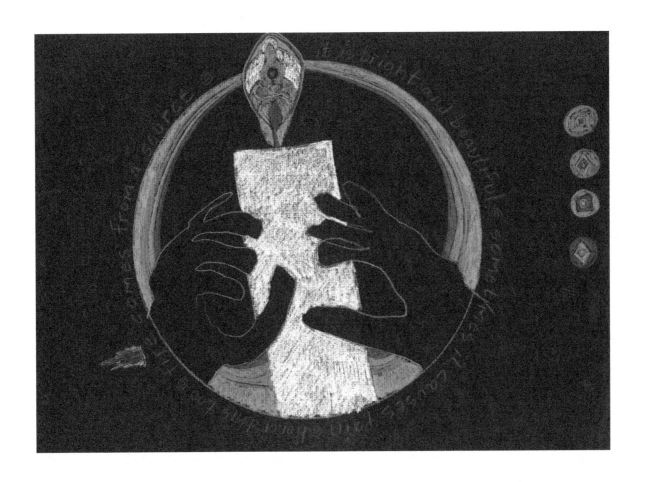

*My soul is a candle that burned away the veil* that kept me in the dark too long.

I want to be the flame, the heat, the light that never goes out.

*My understanding used to be like a stream* - swift, fast, moving. Gathering pieces to carry it along. Washing me clean over and over again. My understanding gets in the way of my love.

N

*Nibble at me* in the smallest of ways. A flicker that could be sun rippling across water.

*No one knows his name* as well as I. Before he was conceived I called him into this world and for this I am joyful.

*No one lives outside the walls of this sacred place, existence* is a dream in an amazing display of color and time. It's full of seasons and desires. Full of hate and despair. Full of hope and madness: An odd lots of mortals and essential beings who do not speak a word of truth.

*No one was cracking the koans* until the blind man told me to look at the moon.

*Not like a lone beautiful bird.* Not like a paired beautiful couple.

Not like you and me, not like anything I've ever known, this need to connect to all.

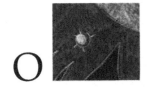 O

*O wondrous creatures* who glide in thin lines of going places for the sake of what? Searching for substance and strength. Searching for the perfect place to rest and make more.

*Okay, I will do it.* I will stop trying to make you like me. I will be kinder, less needed by others. Be gentle with yourself and others. Know how gorgeous your heart behind the iron wall beats.

*On a day* like this I know how old I am. There are reminders in bones and behind eyes.

There are moments I forget the name of you, the name of my ancestors, the places they

came from.


*On the Sabbath, try and make no noise that* isn't needed.
You will get your bread, drink your wine.
You will be met where you stand.
You will not be easily forgotten.

*Once a group of thieves stole a rare diamond* but there was nothing and nowhere it could be

sold. They cut it into pieces and made themselves each a crown that held no power.


*Once I heard two camels talking* I thought I'd gone mad.

The longer I listened the less I understood and then it was time to go home.


*Once I said to God, "How do you teach us?"*

His face became my own.

*One day he did not leave after* he held my gaze and so now he sits at my feet.

We walk together wherever I go.


*One may never have heard the sacred word Christ* as others praise everyday.

Some sit in buildings with steeples, others look up to the redwood trees

and fall to their knees.


*One more song tonight*
before I hope for the land of honey and dreams.
The land of milk and magic.
The promise of words not yet known.
Love not yet expressed.
Desire not yet unleashed.
Please, one more song.


*One night as I walked in the desert* I came upon two camels. So different and so alike.

Their lips pursed and I could swear they were telling one another jokes. With their long

necks lifted and their heads pointing to the stars I knew which road to follow.

*One regret that I am determined not to have* involves a person I've allowed to grow bigger than possible. A short being with short hair, a look of disgust and fear I see as reminders of things long ago. If I throw back my shoulders and sit up straighter maybe I'll remember the trick.

*Only in dream could this happen* - the water in the middle of the bay churns and changes to shadow. Darkness surrounded by light. It's not deeper here I reason when out of the depths comes a creature so grand I can't do a thing. I look as it descends and reaches. I want to call it by a name but there isn't one. It's me and the bigness, the very thing I want so desperately to connect with.

*Only love honors God*
No amount of kneel praying
Or promises
Can compete with Love
Some clutch the rosary
And in the other hand
The throat of those who disagree
Love the only Truth
The only Medicine
The only way to go back Home.

*Our hands imbibe like roots*
Tangled and shallow
Tap and deep
The places we've come from
The web of being you
And me
The crowns of each plant
Reach to the light
I want the very same

*Our union is like this.* The caw-cawing of birds in flight. The calling out. Searching for what will feed us. Wings were lost while time moved on. There is a constant itch in my collarbone, small feathers in our bedding.

P

*Power is safest in a poet's hand*
Broken meters
Lower case i's
Rhyme and rhythm
A hundred plus ways
To say the word Love.

# respect

# Q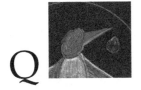

*Quiet yourself*

Before speaking


*Quietly her face spread* like a berry jam on warm sourdough bread.

The sweetness when it hits the roof of the mouth.

The tiny seeds you carry away.


# R

*Remember, God, that we are the plants in your fields.* Us, who bear fruits and flowers. Us, with scabs so the ants eat us alive. Us, with the memory of what to do when spring next opens its eyes.

*Rumi speaking to a crowd muses* and mumbles.

Trying to make sense of what anyone is waiting for.

S

*She caught me off guard when my soul said to me*
Why is your breast swollen?
What is the ache that lives behind it?
Where will you go to remember the truth?
Who will you carry with you? When are you going?

*Since no one really knows anything about God*
why do we guess or search?
Why do we beg or pray?
Why do we lie to ourselves or one another?
Why don't we wake up and love?

*Sing, my tongue; sing my hand*
The song I was born with
What is the meaning, the fuss?
When will the laziness drop away
So only sky and snow-capped mountains
Make sense
A lone loon calls to its own echo
Swims towards the sound of loneliness and love.

*So amazing the choir of* ducks, they ride the ripples wind has left.

Their wet beaks singing praise.

*So fragile this petal the earth* where each glade and blade only want to grow.
Why do we prune anything?
There are some flowers that look more beautiful after their blossoms fall away.
Some whose loss breaks my heart.

# wonder

*So many tears behind these words* — letters almost touching, the hope something might make sense. The desire to reach across a thousand miles or the thin hairline that separates us. The knowing we are all one and the sadness when we forget.

*So precious* the tumbled glass left on the beach. And the slippers worn across the wet grass to watch a deer put its lips to the salt water before it too slips away.

*Some Gods say, the tiny ones* are the real teachers. Open their mouths and cries of pain and squeals of delight come with no thoughts, no regrets, no excuses. We wrap them in flannel blankets their mouths twitching for what might come next as we fall completely and madly in love.

*Some planets rolled in* while I was sleeping.
A galaxy of shimmering stars.
To begin the day with a wish is why I get out of bed.

*Some seeds beneath the earth* wait for perfection. Others wager with no thought to place or time. Either way one lone snail can change the chance of survival.

*Someday you will hear all things applaud your wonder* thunder some will call it as they look to the sky. A clear summer blue pressed and held. Not a cloud in the sky. Who will care when you are gone forever?

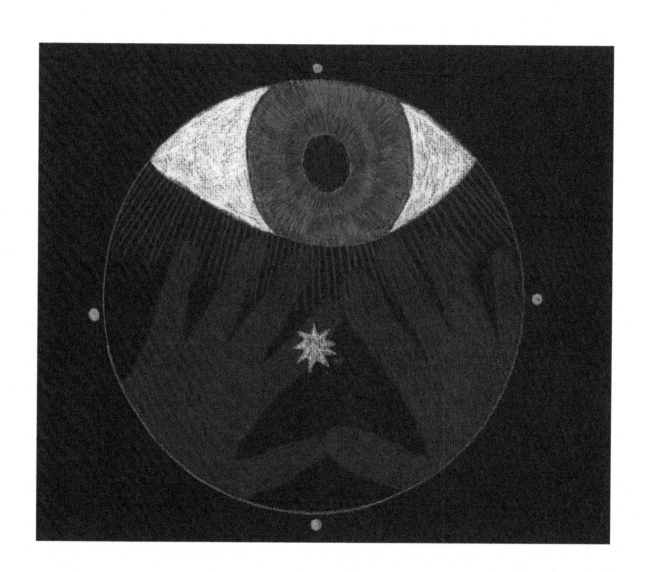

*Something inside said I was a mineral*
*And I was so glad to just be me.*
Part mineral
Part ocean
Air
Nature's people
Part unknown
Every direction
Holds my heart
Every season a place to call now
I am tender I tell you
I feel my heart beating
In the soles of my feet

*Sometimes we think what we are saying about God*
is real, we stand at an altar with open arms
Sing out the names of angels
Stand in rows of pews
Waiting to fall to our knees
Then wait to be invited to stand

*Stuck with another day.*
A box of raisins
a dozen white roses
a song I don't know the words to
How bad can I be?
What can I offer you
that could help you understand
my heart is made of glass
Glass and straw
Straw and dust

*Such love does* exist. I live with it. Light touches the curtains and spreads like butter into

my every pore. I wake up smiling. Bask in the golden glow of newness. Me, with a

name and reason I haven't yet known.

*Tenderly, I now touch all things* before they fall to the earth. Seed to seed. The faith it takes

to go back to where we began. Trust of nourishment and time. Love of the blossom.

*The Christ said to us*
Eat of my body
Drink of my blood
Then the misunderstanding
The waiting for divinity
Unanswered questions
Repeating the Hail Mary


*The earth and sky will open their purse for you*

Throw silver and gold nuggets at your feet

You wouldn't believe it so

The cave is full of treasure.

*The earth looked at him and began to dance*
The breeze turned to wind
The fog to mist
The moon to full
And in the glowing light all creatures turned their heads
To witness a brilliance they
Remembered from another time.


*The experience of something out of nothing* ran through her veins like sap in early spring.

The energy ran up and out. It ran around the wood and settled itself in silver metal

buckets. Later, she would offer you this rich taste of the heart she called hers.


*The force that created the unimaginable splendors*
of a drop of water brought her to her feet.
The reflection it held was all of life.
A minute wonder that insisted more.
Precious and wondrous was the source of the speck.
The thing she searches for even when asleep.

*The grass beneath the tree is content,* do you believe him when he tells you this? His own

head in the lap of you. Luxury, a wicker basket closed to the ants, but inside are morsels

to make you talk. Morsels to make you wonder.


*The limbs of a tree reached down and lifted me*
I whispered to it my name
And asked the same
Maple, oak, fir, alder, cypress
Madrone, manzanita and me
Nothing but a name.
*The moment's depth is greater than that of*
A mountain's divide
Peaks and valleys too close to know
Where one belongs
Why are we born where and when
Who and what do we become
Why not remember, know we are all the same?


*The moon and I* share the same mother. An ancient woman with gold coins for eyes.

When she closes her eyes to sleep stars shine. A path that leads from her to me. Across

an entire ocean she beams.

*The moon was once a moth*
*who ran to her lover*
on paper-weight legs no bigger than a pin.
Two shadowed slivers of desire.
Just by turning on the porch light I became her next.

*The moon was perched like a golden hawk* one wing tucked under the other.

The pale glow was breath in and out. A fine mist of sea foam surrounded it all.

*The rejected lover trembles.* It's the cold wind. It's the long night. It's the wonder of what

might be next or last. I watched the trees shake their gold coins loose, their empty arms

reaching for the sky. Purple shadows crisscrossed, ran down the roads, no worries on

their backs. I wanted to stop and take photographs, worried I'd forget about beauty.

Or death.

*The result of prayer is life*
Is written on the wall in the basement I now live in
Thin letters pressed against bruised stucco
I open a door and think home and yes
I hold a piece of paper to the light
and see tiny grains of rice or dust
I looked for you and when I didn't find you
I ripped a page out of a book
it was thin and again I thought you
I put it in my back pocket
and right away felt heat and hunger.


*The sadness I have caused any face* or heart is the thing I'll take away with me. Who else would open their hands or hearts to hold even a second of anothers pain. Of course, this said, do know that if any one of my children came to me with tears I'd swallow them with no regrets. I'd drink their sorrows like water from a fast running stream. But, please don't tell them. They have all grown to be bigger than me.

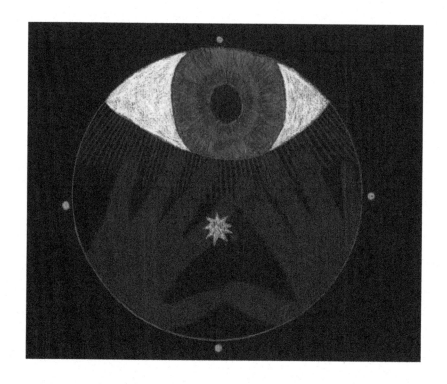

*The sky gave me its heart* bruised and tattered, glorious and full. I took in big breaths and pushed it all aside. Is it really this meager in and out that keeps us alive? The tiny thumping thing in the middle of the chest? Sometimes at night I wonder and can't fall asleep. I know I'm missing so many things and then I can't seem to find my way home.

*The sun hears the fields talking about effort* who said this?
Why?
Fields of amber grains.
Where I live it's fields full of grape vines
and very few other fruits.
It's rows and rows of water to wine.
The vines are trained and traded.
The leaves turn to crimson and gold, the thing I drink.
On the breath of my friends I smell the sour.
My own breath is carrying the night.


*The weight of arrogance is such* a heavy burden.

To feel entitled because you are you.

How heavy is this to carry? Wants you share as needs. Facts and muddled feelings,

I can no longer hold this for you. Before I say yes or no I need to find a place where the

earth is level. I love you just the same but please not now.

*The woman whose speech and actions are the same* is a true healer, warrior, sister. She is the one I will call, the one I invite home. She is the mother of me and my children. She is my daughter and the heart of each of my sons. To walk and talk the truth. To sleep and wake in love. To remind the earth of her preciousness and sacredness while in my own heart I push away fear and sadness. The great Japanese Maple Tree out my window seems to have the answer.

*The wonder of water moving over that rock in the stream* might be the only thing to think about today, tomorrow too, perhaps. It finds its way with a raging grace I'd like to mimic. Swift and agile, no looking back, not much time to plan or worry. Go, I say to myself, go find the way.

*The words Guru, Swami, Super Swami, Master, Teacher, Murshid* make me wonder how there are so many words to say Thanks. If only the teachers of our children also had this one Capital Letter maybe we'd remember to bow to them. We offered apples and now I wonder if there is any thanks at all.

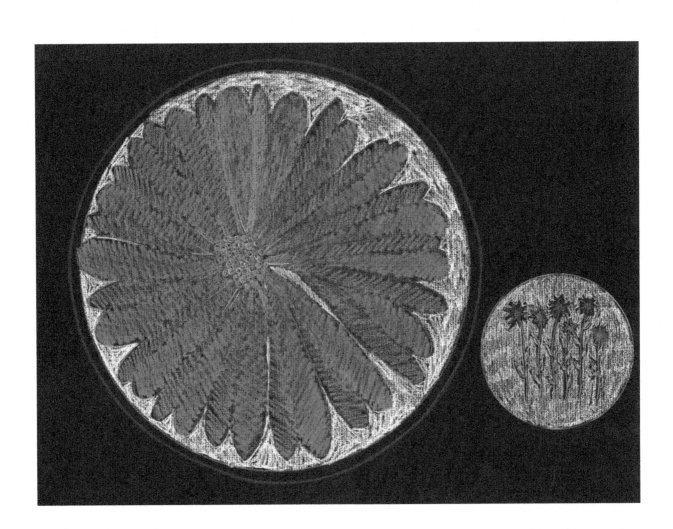

*There are beautiful wild forces within us* all. Every one of us a child born into light, yet for some the embers are never fed or fanned. The cold lump of coal is left in a charred pit and without using it as a tool to spell the very name you were called at birth what can be done? It pains me to think of any helpless babe not being loved.

*There are seasons in the mind* that turn from green to gold, others that throw snow into your mind. Turn it upside down and shake it. Coins and feathers drop to the earth. Flakes that are one of a kind, not that different than you and I. There is spring and new growth. Summer and the shine of long days. Seasons follow the body, and now that I am in the autumn of my life I wish so many things.

*There are so many positions of love.*

I watch a tree drop her leaves. I couldn't look away.

I missed the bus and my lunch. I missed a phone call and the dog's walk. At the base of the marvelous tree there was a pile—colors like a carnival ride sign. I watched a V of geese turn into dust and a single rose lose every pale pink petal. Sometimes it's hard to look away.

*There is a beautiful creature living* inside us each. The purr and howl of our voices are song. We need music and art and poetry. We need food and water and tenderness. The creature within has a million names of its own.

*There is a dog I sometimes take for a walk,* but when truth be told he is the one who takes me. He stops and smells things I wouldn't think of. I imagine he thinks the same of me. He'd like to chase the school bus and the big green and white truck that gathers trash/compost/recycle. He strains at his leash for a mere second until he remembers it was an older life that allowed this, him this tiny thing that wouldn't be heard if he were crunched. He thinks he is bigger than he is, it's starting to rub off on me.

*There is a sword in a museum not far from me* it hangs from a wall the color of fresh blood. There is no other mention of its danger or purpose, no short history, no dates. I think it a reminder of fear and a hate that doesn't have a specific name. It's a sharp, universal reminder of what has been and what could be. Did I tell you it's hanging behind glass thicker than a mile?

*There is dew* and there is DEW, this morning it's the latter. I open the door and a sponge hits my face. Thick like thick. It's fog gone to stew. It's a day on the marvelous coast. My hair will curl, my skin turn to velvet. My walk will wait for later until I can see just far enough to know I haven't yet reached the edge. Others will try to get through it, turn on fog lights, move slowly but I know the best thing to do when one can't see is to wait. If I were blind, like my Aunt Lily, would I too feel of everything?

*These just aren't words you are reading* these are spells and miracles, all witnessed by at least one other. Words in hand don't weigh anything, it's when they enter the heart you feel the worth. To the mind some words are sold, but to the heart always priceless. I don't understand why the painting you do to capture the essence of a poem has a price tag.

*They are always kissing* with their eyes closed. I've watched them for years. I like my eyes and heart wide open when you come that close to me. I like to watch the fleck on your eyes. I like to see the crinkle of your aging skin, knowing how long we have done this one thing. Years fall away and I wonder why we don't get married again. I know places I'd like to celebrate. I know you are the one.

*They are like shy, young school kids* but they are older in years than me. I watched them press their foreheads to one another. A grin on his face. First I thought she the mother, he the son. Now, watching you watch one another I know it isn't the case. She wears a silver cross, it's big. It hangs between her swaying breasts. I've seen her raise it to her lips. Yesterday she offered it to you.

*They can be a great help* these moments of great silence
To drop down into your own well
And remember the bottom doesn't have to be bad
There is mud and darkness
It is here clay is found
I shape myself a bowl a cup
Fashion twisted rungs
And eventually I will climb out
When the rains come
The hole will begin to fill
Not only can I drink
I can swim to the great surface
Oh, for faith, I am so blessed.


*They can be like a sun, words,* lighting up a room, a house, a heart. After a week of overcast skies and truths a love poem with my name on it is a ray of glory. I often wake up and think the word lucky, wonder if it's left over from a dream and then I hear your breathing and remember these limbs are not my own.

*They kiss sometimes when no one is looking* but I see the glow, when I turn to look they are forehead to forehead, pressed together in breath. It happens when they are sitting more often than not as he is so much taller than she. I want to know about the first time they meet. I'm pretty sure it was also their last first time. I think of them wed on the spot, later gathering friends to bear witness to the miracle.

*Three years went by* with no words from you and then last night you stood at my doorway. You are the same all these years later. Things are different; your hair, your weight, my own. But with the dropped angst and no time to find it or sort it out again we hug a year's worth of love and don't say a word. I wonder if you'll be there when I get home tonight.

*Troubled?* by my feet once again. These poor tired vessels that hold me up and move me forward. Yesterday it was three steps back to surprise myself with the sight of a glorious flowering tree outside someone else's window. I wanted it to be mine. There is an itch between my toes that makes me pay attention to where I am going but still I raced to the tree to see if it was real. It didn't pay any attention to me but I feel in love.

Just as I was walking away it tossed me a jewel.

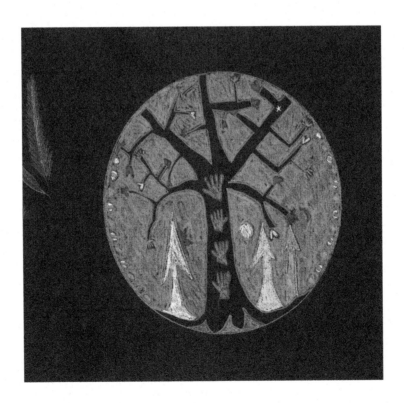

*Truth never frightens* for long. Fear and then anger are quick to move and they take a long slow time to solve or simmer from. Truth is often slow and quiet. It's not as easy to say out loud. It hovers close to veins pulsating with life but to puncture it too fast can be quite a mess. There are so many things I want to say to take care of myself and sometimes it's simply an Amen.

V

*Vulnerable we are, like infants* in the early morning of our lives and days.

My own children slept covered in flannel and love.

They knew love.

They know love.

They are grown ups with loves of their own

and when they walk into a room it makes me want to fly.

*We bless the earth with each step we take.* I remember walking on the beach with my mother, she was bothered by the sound of the surf, it's wasn't her rhythm she told me. I stopped in the damp sand, looked at her hard for one of the first times in my life and laughed. I suggested she think of what/who might be the bigger force. She reminded me she'd always been afraid of water.

*We bloomed in Spring* and flowered throughout the delicious summer. Long days and nights with the smell of seaweed and sweet peas; salt and pepper I say to you, you understand. We grew food to eat and flowers to fill more vases than we own. We wrapped the blossoms in wet newspaper and shared them with anyone we could. The ink came off on our hands and we pressed them down to release any bad news. The comics we saved.

*We know nothing until we know everything* this sounds like something I heard this

morning. I'm on retreat and the saved words of us each has made my breathing easier.

I trust I'll be held up with enough air and goodness that I'll find myself ready to dream.

But, I haven't remembered a one, so I don't know if they've come or passed over me.

Tonight I'll make a special request that you whisper into my sleep a visions of delight.


*"We should rumble," God said.*
Rumble, I ask?
Roar? Thunder? Tussle and roll?
He doesn't care. All he wanted was to get my attention.
I've been distracted by white walls and naked plants.
I've been writing poetry and remembering my name.
In a few hours or a few days I'll try to light up the sky.


*We work so hard to fly* all the flapping about and running so fast. Trying to climb to high

places and check the wind. Our baby wings are soft downy feathers that only look like

they might work. Not yet, not yet. I know there will be a day and when it comes

I wonder if I'll look back.

*What a cruel act to be untruthful.* I know sometimes it seems like the kinder thing to do but it's always hard to keep these stories going. I want to tell you things but I don't. I want to let you go but I don't. I want you to listen, not tell. And when you tell me I want to listen. I am tired in a way that is beyond physical. I want to lie on mossy rocks and be ten years old again; be called for dinner, ring the bell on my bicycle as I ride home to a dinner of frozen fish sticks and french fries. The ketchup a reminder of what is yet to come.

*What could have caused your grip to weaken?* Could it have been the three cords of firewood, moved and stacked? The pulling up of three seasons of vegetables, the turning of soil, and the trimming of the apple trees? Or could it have been the day you took off yesterday, the pages you turned, the drinks you raised? Or could it simply be the weather or your new age?

*What is it you want to change?* Your shoes? Your name? The way you signed the letter to the old friends who are no longer? Once in awhile you really surprise me. I guess it's good to learn mystery from the one you have loved for so long.

*What keeps us alive, what allows us to endure?* Hope, courage, breathe, bees, food, water, love, dreams, courage, family. I am ever so blessed to have it all. Sometimes I fall flat and don't remember how simple compassion is. Sometimes I want to scream NO into the dusk. Into the stink of a low burning fire. Mornings are my best time. I like it when it's dark and then turns light as if I had anything to do with it.

*What kind of God would He be* if he turned his back on the mean-spirited? If we turned prisons into retreats centers and feed people good food, served whipping cream on warm cakes, don't you think folks would come back for more? I get hungry from smells coming from a kitchen where things are made with love. I'd work for a place at that table.

*What part of heaven did she come from?* Angels from up high, where was she born,where did she die? Maybe more important than how died or why but when? When in her precious life? When death is named untimely whose eyes and heart are the ones left behind? A child with cancer, a car crash on the way to get eggs, an airplane on the way to holiday. Why and when? How many people get to say goodbye?

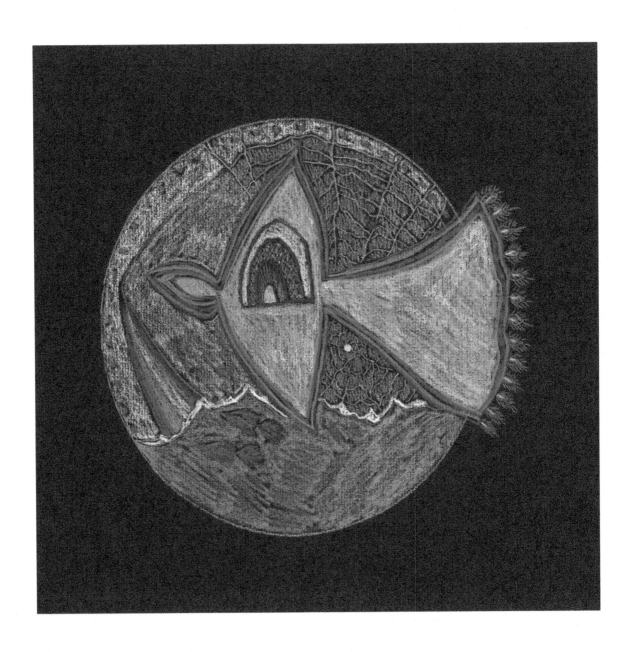

*What will our children do in the morning?* So many of us asked this to one another this past week, but for some it's an every single day question with no answer good enough to tell. No breakfast for them, no shoes for their feet, no education or health care, and water that makes them sick. Perhaps a great luxury for us to be so worried about the next four years when we have food in our bellies and homes.

*What would a buried man alive do?*

Dirt under the nails already.

An entire life working to stay to above ground.

*When God says to God, "Where are you?"* What then can I ask of myself or you? Where am I? What are we doing here? This one precious life and these silly moments of unrest and fear, the thinking I can change a stolen minute of what is to be. If I can live and remember to enter each new room in awe and with reverence so many things are allowed to drop away, like rain on the window. The trickle of release.

*When he touches me I clutch the sky's sheets* it's like this in my bed. I sleep with someone

I truly love. Is adore understood? Can I use entwined as a noun? On our front porch we

have growing a pretty Mexican Bell Vine though I know it was born with a fancier

name. Magenta flowers hang from its mess of trellis. It wraps itself around the closest

thing. This is me reaching for you.

*When I was the stream,*
*when I was the* river
you jumped right in.

The cold water took your breath away,
that too was me.

I've saved all these extra inhales.
Someday one us of might need them.

*When my mouth touched His I became invisible.* This very primitive and expansive kiss of

life then death. So many things and ones to live for. So many more to die for.

*When were you last really happy?*
What if I add a few words and see now how you answer?
When were you last really happy with your own self?
What were you doing? Can you go back there right now?


*When you recognize beauty* does it have a name, a color, smell, a memory, a sound, a

taste? What does it look like. Take up the pen, the paint, the phone, your voice.

Don't ever forget this moment.


*When your soul was born* so too was I. All our lives leading up the moment of our

connection, the union of us, and we were doubly blessed. A young one came from us.

He is one of the prophets of Love.


*Where am I going on this glorious journey?* To gather herbs for tea. Sometimes the journey

is simple. But once I step outside things may and will change.

A hummingbird takes my attention, a fat-bellied robin taking a morning bath, now two,

then three. All splashing water out of the bath. I think I see them grinning.

*Why not look at the beauty* of writing you a Love letter, even if not a single letter gets pressed to the paper, the paper itself is for you. Sometimes I give you the first eggs peeled. Sometimes not.

*Why think God has not touched everything?* I answer the question by asking you the same. I have my own thoughts and beliefs, as do you. And though you go each week to His big house and I do not we are the same. We are dust and earth, sin and joy. We are the rose and its bloodied thorn. We are the dirt it grows in and the sun that asks it to blossom.

*Wisdom is* prevalent in all things.
It is so unbelievably hard to trust every moment. Why?
How many ways and times must we told we are loved?
How much suffering must we endure before we say Amen.

*With a begging bowl in hand a man with amnesia* returned again and again to the kitchen of this great house. For these treasures I too might be willing to lose my mind. I am fed in all ways from this place of pureness and silence.

*With all humility* I ask what it is you mean by saying no more poems are needed? Your poems, my poems, poems of suffering and courage, poems of joy and sorrow? I want you to take it back, say you never meant it. Change the verbiage to all and more. Throw them out like confetti or rice on the bride of each moment. Wake up and tell the world how much you love it. How much you love me.

*With passion pray,* with passion dance, sing, write, speak, love.
With passion grow up and grow older.
Grow yourself younger.
Crawl to the altar of your own precious life.
Sit on the velvet cushion and feel the bottoms of your feet
And heart.
Everywhere, everywhere there is beauty.
A dead branch sitting in a pot in the corner of the room
Shows its beauty as a thin shadow.
Don't stop looking.
Don't stop hoping.

*Would any seed take root if it had not believed* the rains would come. All its life it has lived for so little. Asked not much. After three days of rain an absurd green haze begins waking up the others. Drought is a time to remember all the things we've lost.

*Would not the sun have lost its mind* if the moon did not relieve it on occasion. It too welcomes the rain. As does the darkness we call evening. The sun works harder than most and its reward is what?

*Would you come if someone called you* and wouldn't leave their name, only saying urgent.

It's a voice I almost remember from long ago. I'm sure you'll want to speak. But, what if

it is the one we call death and you are happily trimming the crowded irises.

Maybe I should hang up the line.

Y

*You are sitting in a wagon* with your feet dangling off the back

you are too big for this I want to say to you

but with your hand and smile you call me over.

It's a red wagon the rust has eaten parts of its heft.

The holes are rough lace against the back of my thigh.

We lie back together, there is no room for any of this

but still we see a blazing shooting stars

and just like that we are old friends again.

*You have not danced so badly, my dear.* You have not stepped on my toes any more than I have stepped on yours. When I was little it was the tops of slippery leather shoes. My grandfather's pipe tobacco blown onto the top of my head. Everything grew warm. It's when I first knew there really was a God.

*You let my suffering cease* for in those moments I heard the song of birds and the rumble of waves. The ringing in my ears that I try to, but can't, embrace as bird song will one day make me mad. The sirens are high. The need to shut them out. But like the snoring of the woman who I now know is compromised I think alas, alas, it's such a miracle to hear anything at all.


*You might hear the beautiful shout of "Geronimo"*
though I know not what this means.
Is it the felling of a big tree?
The run to battle?
The calling of the child to supper?
So many ways to know something.


*You might quiet the whole world for a second* for me,
But we have already spoken of this
There is silence
And there is quiet,
Is there nothing in between?

*You should act more responsibly, God* is watching. He's over there in the Japanese Maple

tree handing out golden tokens to heaven. He's dropped lots of them on the ground and

I'm not afraid to gather them. I'll put them in vases and baskets. I'll iron them between

pieces of waxed paper. I'll send you as many as you'd like.


*You taught your songs to the birds first*

and they then shared it with the world.

I know people who can sing and make the hairs on arms rise.

All my life I wanted to be able to do this one thing for you.

I open my mouth and shut it again.

I honor the birds for so many reason.

Voice and wings?

How did they become some blessed?

*Your body is a divine stream* and I am a lone fish hoping for nothing but time.

Z

*Zeal, where does it come from?*
Zeal, where does it go?
The passion of passion
Is the way to be.

Patty Joslyn moved back to Mendocino County, California, in 2012 from Vermont where she worked primarily in End-Of-Life Care. She is fascinated with both death and birth as passages into new realms. As a writer she has been published in El Calendario de Todos Santos, poetsonline.org, VOYA, (Voices of Youth Advocates) Tupelo Press-30/30 Project-March 2015, and several anthologies. She has been a guest presenter at many events. Patty has eight self-published chapbooks. She and her husband share four (wonderful) grown children.

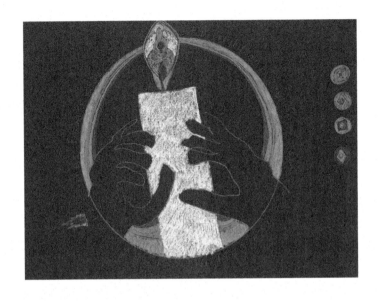

with thanks

## intentions from a few of the drawings

 Dear Spirit, Please reveal a perfect symbol to honor holy origin.

Dear Spirit, please reveal to me a symbol of holy faith, strength, and being.

Dear Spirit, please reveal a symbol to open me to holy hope, harmony and law. Trust my true nature and afford me spiritual surrender.

Dear Spirit, please reveal an image to help me trust and to to be truthful.

Dear Spirit, please reveal to me the 'perfect' symbol to call upon healing for myself and others.

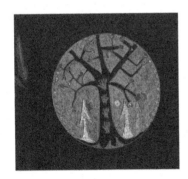

Dear Spirit, please reveal a symbol of balance and truth.

CPSIA information can be obtained
at www.ICGtesting.com
Printed in the USA
BVOW05s1243280217

477353BV00015B/45/P